# THINGS PARAPROFESSIONALS Really WANT TO Say But Can't

# Test Your Colors

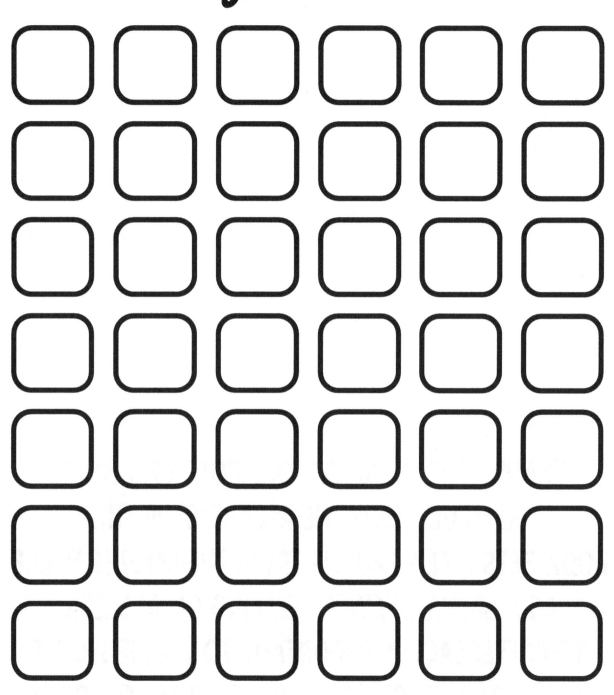

THANKS FOR CHOOSING Our COLORING BOOK.
WE TRULY HOPE THE RECIPIENT OF THIS
BOOK GETS A FEW LAUGHS FROM THE QUOTES INSIDE.
AS A SMALL BUSINESS SELLING ON AMAZON,
YOUR FEEDBACK IS IMPORTANT TO US. WE WOULD
APPRECIATEIT IF YOU COULD take A MINUTE TO POST
AN HONEST REVIEW ON AMAZON.